"I genuinely appreciate this book. It is a thoughtful synthesis of scriptural exhortations with what should be common sense. It seems that sometimes when it comes to evangelism and apologetics, Christians feel the need to take on a different persona and become unnecessarily confrontational and--to put it crassly--obnoxious. When Christian students ask me about how to handle the pressures that may come with attending a secular university, my first piece of advice is always, "Don't make a spectacle of yourself!" This book takes us one step beyond such elementary exhortations and gives us a positive, helpful approach to the Christian's encounter with non-Christian thought and those who think it. A real strength of the book is that it is grounded on biblical teaching rather than on the latest insights from the ever-changing insights of psychology, communication theory, and similar disciplines. Clearly, even if they are right in their descriptive reports, they cannot provide an obligatory, prescriptive standard for our behavior in the same way that the Bible does. Whether one agrees or disagrees with some of the fine points of Trevor Slone's exegesis, as long as we derive our thinking from scripture, we cannot go wrong in the long run. I really like the way Trevor ends each chapter with some practical "take-aways." Unfortunately, in many Christian circles the "practical application" has been the entire content of teaching materials. However, the proper reaction to this "behavioral modification" approach is not to dispense with the practical side altogether, and Trevor does a good job highlighting the specific actions that should arise out of the passages he treats. Timely--biblical--practical. A good combination."

- Dr. Winfried Corduan, Professor Emeritus of Philosophy and Religion, Taylor University; author of "In the Beginning God."

Doing Apologetics Without the Need for Apology:

Biblical Principles for Confrontational Relationality

Trevor Ray Slone

This book is dedicated to one of my Ratio Christi students at Kansas State University, Marjory Dunlap, as she is the one who brought the topic of this book to my attention, and for that I am forever grateful!

3

Table of Contents

<u>Acknowledgements</u>

First and foremost I need to thank my wife for proofreading this manuscript. She is one of the smartest people I know, and she is also an excellent asset to have when one is in need of a critical eye and a keen mind. Also, I need to thank my students from my Sunday school class at church and my Ratio Christi students at Kansas State University for enduring my often inadequate representation of the information I wish to convey, especially as I developed the ideas and information set forth in this book. I also would like to thank my friends in the apologetics world, Dr. Norman Geisler, Dr. Winfried Corduan, Dr. Donald Williams, Kerby Anderson, Dr. Bill Roach, Dr. Phil Fernandes, and many others who have influenced me in this area of study and have been a great encouragement to me last several years, especially at our annual International Society of

Christian Apologetics (ISCA) conferences. It is an absolute blessing to be a part of such a great organization that stands first and foremost for the inerrancy of Scripture and for doing apologetics in a way that is winsome, intellectually stimulating, and gospel driven.

Preface

As I was beginning my Ratio Christi Christian ministry at Kansas State University earlier this year, one of the first things I decided was that I was going to only teach things that my students were concerned with, rather than simply teaching whatever I decided I wanted to teach. So, each week I asked my students what they wanted me to talk about during the meeting the following week. One Thursday, a few weeks into the ministry one of my students emailed me and asked me if I could discuss how to interact with people when doing apologetics in a way that is winsome. I immediately realized that this is a very pertinent issue and so I decided not only to teach on that topic the next Thursday night at our meeting, but I also taught on the same topic in my Sunday morning Sunday school class that next week.

This book is an assimilation of that information, along with a few more passages that I thought were relevant to the topic at hand. This book is not meant to be exhaustive in nature but rather it is meant to cover the basic elements of what it takes to interact with people in a manner worthy of both Christ and the gospel. In this book you will discover first and foremost that the purpose of apologetics is evangelism and not argumentation or simply proving that you are smarter than someone. If you take away nothing else from this book, I pray that it is this at the very least.

In Christ,

Trevor Ray Slone

<u>Chapter 1: 2 Corinthians 10:1-5</u>

"I, Paul, myself entreat you, by the meekness and gentleness of Christ—I who am humble when face to face with you, but bold toward you when I am away!— [2] *I beg of you that when I am present I may not have to show boldness with such confidence as I count on showing against some who suspect us of walking according to the flesh.* [3] *For though we walk in the flesh, we are not waging war according to the flesh.* [4] *For the weapons of our warfare are not of the flesh but have divine power to destroy strongholds.* [5] *We destroy arguments and every lofty opinion raised against the knowledge of God, and take every thought captive to obey Christ." – 2 Corinthians 10:1-5 (ESV)*

This is a fairly lengthy passage with a lot of information packed into it, so let's dive right in and get started! We will be going through some portions of this passage more thoroughly than others, but I have included the context as the passage makes more sense that way. Some may notice that I have excluded verse six from this passage. That is because, although it is technically the end of the overall thought in this section of the chapter, there are some unnecessarily potentially burdensome (time-consuming) aspects involved in tying it into the first five verses, especially relative to the

purpose of this book, and so I thought it best to simply

point that out and not actually address the interpretation

of verse six in this book. Although all of Scripture is

essentially valid and meaningful, verse six is unnecessary

for the purpose of this book which is intended to be a

small, accessible resource for those seeking practical

answers to the question of how to interact with others

when doing apologetics.

Verse 1

*"I, Paul, myself entreat you, by the meekness and gentleness of Christ—
I who am humble when face to face with you, but bold toward you
when I am away!"*

Here, at the outset of the chapter, Paul the

Apostle comes to us in "the meekness and gentleness of

Christ." Without getting too carried away with this part

of the passage, let it just be pointed out that Paul is

"entreating" us to do something that, as we will see

throughout the remainder of this chapter, he himself is

doing with us in this passage, namely being bold in his speech and manner when away, yet humble when face to face with those of his day. This seems to indicate that humility and boldness are separate and possibly even opposed to or opposite from one another, but this is not actually the case. Paul here is simply indicating that, as many of us have probably realized, it is easier, and often times more efficient, to be bold in our long distance interactions with others when we are serious. By contrast, the facial mannerisms and body language that accompanies face to face interaction often lessens the need to speak in a more bold fashion. So, we are to be bold in content, and sometimes, when necessary, in mannerism, but always humble, whether in the presence or absence of boldness. For humility is ultimately remembering and maintaining an active awareness of one's wholehearted insufficiency apart from Christ, and

11

there is nothing about boldness or any other potentially necessary attribute that negates the necessity of such a mindset.

Verse 2

"I beg of you that when I am present I may not have to show boldness with such confidence as I count on showing against some who suspect us of walking according to the flesh."

In this second verse we see that Paul actually does not wish to show much boldness, and that a more extreme type of boldness is reserved in Paul's mind and heart for those situations in which it is necessary to confront falsity and inappropriate opposition. This shows us that, while at times it is okay to be bold when face to face with others, for the most part, and under normal circumstances, it is better to remain as humble as possible. Again, this is not to say that we cannot be bold and humble at the same time, but here Paul's mannerisms are in view rather than what he specifically has to say. We do not need to doubt the fact that Paul was virtually always bold in the content of what he had to say, if we consider speaking the truth without apology boldness, but at the same time Paul tells us in this verse that, generally speaking, he is humble when face to face with others. Hence we can draw the inference that Paul was usually humble in character and mannerisms while also being bold in the content of his speech.

We can also gather from this verse that Paul is against the idea of walking according to the flesh, i.e. living habitually in sin, especially as a believer, for he indicates that he is boldly against this idea that some are purporting of him. And if Paul was against it, then we should be too, considering the fact that this concept lines up wholly with the teachings of Jesus and the rest of Scripture.

Verse 3
"For though we walk in the flesh, we are not waging war according to the flesh."

13

In this third verse we see a slight change in wording from "according to the flesh" to "in the flesh." Now to be sure there are some passages in Scripture that when using the phrase "in the flesh" is referring to sin, but this is not the case here. Rather "flesh" in this verse is used to refer to one of its other main connotations, namely "skin" or "humanity," and so here Paul is simply saying that although we walk as humans, our ultimate fight is not with humans.

Verse 4

"For the weapons of our warfare are not of the flesh but have divine power to destroy strongholds."

Here in verse four we see that our "weapons," that is, that which we utilize to defeat the opposing forces and win the ultimate battle that the previous verse tells us is not against humanity, are NOT of the flesh either. This makes perfect sense, for using fleshly, or human weapons to defeat non-fleshly, or spiritual enemies, wouldn't make much sense would it? Also, in this verse, we can infer that if our battle weapons are not physical then they must be spiritual, as that is the only other option. These spiritual weapons are primarily the Armor of God referred to by Paul in Ephesians chapter 6, but the particulars of those weapons are not pertinent to our discussion here. The main thing to take from this verse is that these spiritual weapons have *divine power* to destroy strongholds.

Now, if our battle is not against humanity, but rather against spiritual forces, such as the devil and his fallen angels, and our weapons are of a spiritual nature and have not just power, but divine power to destroy strongholds, then it is safe to say that it follows that the strongholds mentioned in this passage are also ultimately of a spiritual nature, for the idea of the "spiritual rather than the physical" is prevalent throughout this passage.

So, this means that our ability to defeat the devil, which would include defeating his spiritual hold on the souls of non-believers, is completely and one hundred percent dependent on our spiritual weapons. Now, our spiritual weapons and our use of them, are guided by the Holy Spirit, and so it is ultimately the Holy Spirit, and not us personally, who are responsible for and able to bring someone to a saving knowledge of Christ. This is the ultimate defeating of the devil and his spiritual "stronghold" on non-believers. It is vitally important to remember this, for we must not forget that no matter how solid our apologetic arguments are, they are still ultimately referring to spiritual things in some sense, and those things can only truly be understood and accepted with the help and guidance of the Holy Spirit (relative to a salvific understanding and acceptance). So don't get too beat up mentally or emotionally when you don't seem to be able to get through to some people, for there is a spiritual war involved, and it is not and cannot be won simply by rational argumentation.

Verse 5

"We destroy arguments and every lofty opinion raised against the knowledge of God, and take every thought captive to obey Christ."

In this final verse of the passage that we are here looking at, we see that Paul is in fact talking about ideas that are contrary to the God and the Bible (i.e. the knowledge of God). More specifically, when we look at the second part of this verse we see that the purpose of destroying these arguments and ideas that oppose God is to "obey Christ." This is key, so listen closely (read carefully) here: APOLOGETICS IS NOT ABOUT ARGUMENTATION, BUT ABOUT PLEASING, FOLLOWING, AND LEADING PEOPLE TO CHRIST! True, we must sometimes use various arguments in this process, but the ultimate goal of apologetics is not to win

17

the argument, but, at the risk of using a theologically

inadequate cliché, "win the soul."

Practical Take-a-ways

- **Be bold when necessary.**

- **Always be humble, even when being bold.**

- **Remember that our fight is not with humanity but rather with the devil and his demons.**

- **It is ultimately up to the Holy Spirit, not us, whether others accept and/or agree with our arguments that point toward Christ and the truthfulness of Christianity, especially in a way that leads to a salvific understanding of the faith.**

- **The purpose of apologetics is to lead people to Christ, not to win arguments or demonstrate how smart you are.**

Chapter 2: 2 Timothy 2:23-26

"Have nothing to do with foolish, ignorant controversies; you know that they breed quarrels. [24] And the Lord's servant must not be quarrelsome but kind to everyone, able to teach, patiently enduring evil, [25] correcting his opponents with gentleness. God may perhaps grant them repentance leading to a knowledge of the truth, [26] and they may come to their senses and escape from the snare of the devil, after being captured by him to do his will." - *2 Timothy 2:23-26 (ESV)*

This is a passage that deals specifically with why it is important not to dabble in worthless talk. It is one thing to talk about the weather or the news as a form of small talk so that you can converse with others in an attempt to build rapport, but sometimes we just get caught up in meaningless discussions, such as what a square circle would look like or how big a baby pink unicorn would be at birth. Okay, obviously I am being a bit silly here, but my point, I am sure, has nevertheless been made. The fact is, however, that this passage, when kept in context as we will see in a moment, is talking more about avoiding things that lead people away from

Christ, rather than specific topics of discussion per se.

(As a side note, this passage is intended for church leadership, but the principles, being that they are somewhat moral in nature, can be seen as universal in scope, although the church leadership will certainly be held to a higher degree of liability regarding their adherence to such principles.)

Verse 23

"Have nothing to do with foolish, ignorant controversies; you know that they breed quarrels."

This verse tells us that we are to not only avoid, but literally have "nothing to do with" controversies that are foolish. In other words, we are to completely and utterly avoid all types and forms of illegitimate discussions. Notice, however, that particular topics are not mentioned here, nor are they necessarily even in question in this verse. Rather, the term "controversies" is used. This indicates, that rather than the topic itself, what is being done with the topic, such as how it is being addressed, or perhaps what aspect of the topic is being discussed and in what way, or for what end is at issue. For instance, something like a baby pink unicorn may not actually exist, but it is not inherently evil or anti-biblical to talk about it. If you are using it as an analogy to explain something, like I did in the above paragraph, then the topic is being discussed in a coherent and rational manner. However, if you are arguing with someone about how big that unicorn will be when it is six months old for the express purpose of entertainment or just to waste time talking about something interesting, then this is not at all ultimately productive relative to leading people to Christ. So unless there is some higher purpose (actual purpose; not just an excuse/nominal purpose) in mind, such as building rapport to become better friends with someone so that they might be more open to hearing the gospel message from you in the future, then discussing something for the purpose of entertainment alone is inappropriate and a waste of time at best, and a down-right sin at worst. I know this sounds harsh, but we must always remember that our time is precious and that every moment we waste has the potential to bring the non-believers around us one step closer to Hell!

Verse 24

"And the Lord's servant must not be quarrelsome but kind to everyone, able to teach, patiently enduring evil,"

This verse tells us that not only are we not to be contentious about things that do not matter, but more specifically that we are supposed to be kind to "everyone." Wait! What? Everyone? Yes, EVERYONE! But what about the rude people and the Atheists and the Satanists and all the other people who disagree with us? Quite simply, everyone obviously includes them too.

This means that we are supposed to be cordial, pleasant mannered, and polite to all those that we come into contact with in any way, whether they agree with us or not. Listen, the fact of the matter is that the vast majority of the people that you come into contact with, if you are living a truly missional lifestyle, are going to disagree with you about something, and many of them will disagree with you about a lot of things, but your job as a believer is not to convince them to agree with you, rather it is to show them that you love and care about them in whatever way you can. This includes, but is certainly not limited to, praying for them and communicating the gospel message in a way that they can comprehend, which also means being able to answer any questions and/or objections that they may have to the Christian faith and message. The latter part of that last sentence flows into the next part of this verse, which tells us that the Lord's servant, i.e. every believer, MUST be able to teach. This is, I am sure, eye opening to many of you who are reading this. After all, the gift of teaching is only given to some, right? Well, maybe teaching in a professional sense, but the basic concept of teaching can be and is bound up in sharing the gospel with others, and this is what we all as believers have been called to do in the Great Commission (Matt. 28:18-20).So at least on a basic level we are all, as believers, called and commanded (hence the term "must") to teach others. Also, and finally regarding this verse, all Christians must patiently endure evil, especially when we are teaching (based on the immediate context of this verse and phrase). This means that while many times we will be ridiculed and put down, and even verbally and physically abused for sharing our faith, whether through basic evangelism or apologetic evangelism (ultimately doing Christian apologetics is evangelism; see 1 Peter 3:15a), we nevertheless are required, again via the term "must" in the first part of this verse, to endure it and anything else that is thrown our way that is not Christ-like, with patience, and also humility (remember chapter 1 of this book!).

Verses 25 and 26

"correcting his opponents with gentleness. God may perhaps grant them repentance leading to a knowledge of the truth, [26] and they may come to their senses and escape from the snare of the devil, after being captured by him to do his will."

These final two verses of this passage are lumped together here because the second verse is the completion of the thought in the first verse, even more so than these two verses are a completion of the thought of the previous two verses. Now, these two verses tell us that, first of all, we are to correct our opponents with gentleness. What does this mean? Several things; first it means that we are to actually correct those who oppose us, or more specifically those who oppose our teachings, for remember that the last chapter of this book pointed out that our battle is not with humanity or of the flesh. Also, the way in which we are to correct our opponents is expressly stated in verse 25, namely with *gentleness*. This means that when we are in the process of correcting our opponents we are to be calm, collected, and meek, even if we are being bold in correcting them. Neither must we forget to be humble, for humility, while not a necessary attribute of gentleness, is nevertheless a standard and winsome attribute, which ties clearly into the goal of being gentle, which is essentially to win over one's opponent, at least in some sense.

Why are all of these things in this passage important? Look at the rest of it! It says in verse 25b-26 that God may use your gentle, meek, humble, patient, teaching spirit to bring these individuals into an eternal state of grace! WOW! Wouldn't that be GREAT!

Practical Take-a-ways

- **Completely and utterly avoid worthless discussions, for your time is far too precious to waste on such things (such <u>things</u>, not people; remember that!).**

- **All Christians must be not only willing but able to teach, and to teach, at minimum, the gospel message.**

- **We must be kind to everyone, no matter how they may treat us.**

- **We must be patient in our endurance of evil of all types.**

- **We must correct those who oppose our truly Christian teachings. (This involves the essentials only, remember that also, as the Scriptures elsewhere make it clear that we are not to quarrel over non-essential issues. It is fine to *discuss* them in the proper context however**

(Romans 14!))

- **In doing all of this, the Lord may well bring our opponents to a saving knowledge of Himself!**

Chapter 3: James 3:9-12

"With it we bless our Lord and Father, and with it we curse people who are made in the likeness of God. [10] From the same mouth come blessing and cursing. My brothers, these things ought not to be so. [11] Does a spring pour forth from the same opening both fresh and salt water? [12] Can a fig tree, my brothers, bear olives, or a grapevine produce figs? Neither can a salt pond yield fresh water." – James 3:9-12 (ESV)

This passage is talking about the infamous tongue, that with which we often both bless and curse people in the same sentence, thereby proving our inadequacy regarding the perfect standard that God has set for us. This passage is very important, for many times, and probably more often than not, we fail to realize that while we may not intend to be disrespectful, we nevertheless come across that way to those with whom we are conversing. Also, when we are attempting to actually be rude, we seldom realize that we in fact should not be doing so.

Verse 9

"With it we bless our Lord and Father, and with it we

curse people who are made in the likeness of God."

This first verse of this particular passage tells us that we use our tongue not only to bless God, which is certainly noble and just, but also to curse humans. This is a problem for several reasons, but the main one in view in this verse is the fact that those people who we are disrespecting are made in God's image. That is, we are hypocrites, for we claim to love God but at the same time we are rude and disrespectful to those who are made in His likeness and image. We all need to remember this as we approach people and situations with apologetics, as we have a tendency to be rude when arguing with people and that is counterproductive to the apologetic task, which necessarily includes evangelism. We must always uphold and actively recognize the dignity and self-worth of those we come in contact with as those who bear God's image, as anything less is to disrespect God Himself.

Verse 10

"From the same mouth come blessing and cursing. My brothers, these things ought not to be so."

This verse reiterates what was just discussed in the above paragraph. We curse and bless with the same mouth, thereby making us all hypocrites on a fundamental level. Now this does not mean that all Christians are complete hypocrites, as many people claim, but rather that we need to be all the more cautious as to how we speak and what we say (whether that language be audible or not), for our witness, and therefore the furtherance of the Kingdom of God and the gospel message depend on it. Also, as the second part of this verse states, the fact that we both bless and curse with the same mouth should not be the case. This does not mean that we should rather curse through some other mode, but that instead we should not curse anyone at all.

It also must not be overlooked that James here uses the phrase "my brothers" to start the latter sentence in this verse, which indicates that he is especially talking to believers, for after all, non-believers cannot truly bless God in the first place, and so this exhortation in this passage is specifically, not just generally, speaking to believers, although the principle of speaking both good and evil simultaneously is a universal one that applies to all people to be sure.

Verse 11

"Does a spring pour forth from the same opening both fresh and salt water?"

This verse poses a question that, when truly considered, brings up a very pertinent yet humbling point, for the answer to this question is obviously "No," for once salt enters the water it necessarily becomes salt water, and the absence of such salt, essentially, in this context, makes it fresh water. The water must either be one or the other, but it CANNOT be both. What does this mean in terms of life and apologetics though? Well, first of all it means that the legitimacy of our intentions are made clear through our words and the information that we convey, for after all, it was just said that we do actually bless and curse with the same tongue, so this passage cannot simply be saying that we must either do one or the other, at least not on a fundamental level. Sure, on a surface level, that is, at face value, we can both bless and curse with the same tongue, but on a deeper level we see through this verse that in reality only the blessing or the curse is actually legitimate, for it is true that prior to the mixing of salt and fresh water there is both, just as there is a blessing before a curse or a curse before a blessing, but once they have both been established, only one may prevail, for they cannot both exist at the same time and place and in the same sense. So, as we go about our apologetic ministry, we must remember that even if we say the truth and all the right things, if we do so in a manner that is unbecoming or crass, we are no longer speaking for God, but for ourselves and for the opposing side, for to be rude is almost inevitably to lead people away, rather than toward Christ, and the purpose of apologetics, as stated earlier, is to lead people to Christ!

Verse 12

"Can a fig tree, my brothers, bear olives, or a grapevine produce figs? Neither can a salt pond yield fresh water."

Again we see here in this final verse of this passage the phrase "my brothers," which indicates that James is speaking to fellow believers in the Lord primarily. James here asks another question similar to the previous one, but this time the topic is vines. Can one type of tree bear another type of fruit? Well, leaving modern agricultural technology (which was not available in ancient times when James was writing his epistle) aside, the answer is an unmitigated "No!" What does this mean? It means the same thing that the question regarding the water discussed above means; that we cannot legitimately support or uphold both good and evil at the same time and in the same sense. We must pick one or the other. This is proved by the end of this verse, which starts with the term "neither," which indicates that the answer to the previous set of questions is negative, i.e. "No." But why does James ask several questions, obviously rhetorical, about the same thing, and then actually answer the questions in the end, referring back to the first question? Several reasons come to mind. First, this is a popular literary strategy that is often used to emphasize a point, thereby indicating that the author believes that it is extremely important. Also, by going back at the end of the passage and answering the first question, after already having

have asked another question, the author ties the

questions together, along with the already obvious

answer, to show that it is all ultimately one thought, or

rather it is all about the same issue.

Practical Take-a-ways

- We must be very careful as to how we speak, for we either curse or bless, but we cannot do both at the same time and in the same sense.

- All people are made in the image of God.

- Blessings cannot breed evil, and curses cannot breed good (apart from divine grace and providence).

<u>Chapter 4: Various Passages In Proverbs</u>

"The wise of heart will receive commandments, but a babbling fool will come to ruin." –Proverbs 10:8 (ESV)

"Whoever isolates himself seeks his own desire; he breaks out against all sound judgment. A fool takes no pleasure in understanding, but only in expressing his opinion."- Proverbs 18:1-2 (ESV)

"The one who states his case first seems right, until the other comes and examines him." – Proverbs 18:17 (ESV)
"Do not speak in the hearing of a fool, for he will despise the good sense of your words." – Proverbs 23:9 (ESV)
"Answer not a fool according to his folly, lest you be like him yourself." – Proverbs 26:4 (ESV)
"A man of wrath stirs up strife, and one given to anger causes much transgression." – Proverbs 29:22 (ESV)

It is a well-known fact that the book of Proverbs

contains a lot of very insightful information. There is

much in it about wisdom and many other topics. In this

chapter we are going to review several of the passages

in Proverbs that talk about interacting with both

information and individuals. There are a few more verses

discussed in this chapter than the other chapters so bear

with me and I guarantee you won't be disappointed in

the end.

Proverbs 10:8

"The wise of heart will receive commandments, but a babbling fool will come to ruin."

In this passage we see that the first part of the verse discusses those who are wise, that is the wise of heart. Section (a) of this verse indicates that those who are wise will receive commandments, that is, they will heed and obey them, rather than shun and/or ignore them. This is an important concept to remember, for the Lord truly has given us many commandments, and he expects us to follow and heed each and every one of them. For instance, one of God's commandments is for us not to bear false witness against our neighbor. This comes into play regarding apologetics when and if we create strawman arguments. In other words, when we argue against points that our opponents do not truly believe or are not arguing, then in a sense we are saying that they are in fact arguing these points and bearing false witness against them. Put another way, we should be careful to understand our opponent's position, which often requires asking them questions, such as to clarify their position so that we may better understand where they're coming from, and by doing so we may avoid misunderstanding and thereby misrepresenting them in their position.

As for the second part of this verse, it is in direct contrast to the first part. Section (b) of this passage indicates that a babbling fool, or rather one who does not heed and receive commandments, as can be inferred per the contrast with section (a) of the verse, will come to ruin. In short this means that, one, those who do not heed commandments, that is God's commandments, are babbling fools, or the equivalent thereof; and two, those who are indeed the equivalent of babbling fools will come to ruin, that which is both ultimately undesirable and completely and utterly unpleasant. This reminds us that we must be careful to heed and obey God's commandments, and that in doing so we will avoid an untimely and unpleasant demise.

Proverbs 18:1-2

"Whoever isolates himself seeks his own desire; he breaks out against all sound judgment. A fool takes no pleasure in understanding, but only in expressing his opinion."

In the first part of this passage we see that he who isolates himself seeks his own desire, that is, he is selfish and unrighteous. This is an issue obviously, as we are all called to be concerned with God's will and God's glory rather than our own. We also see here that it is inappropriate to isolate ourselves, which means that we are to necessarily interact with others. This is in direct contrast to the idea that our faith is merely personal and ultimately has nothing to do with anyone else. After all, the Great Commission necessitates that we interact with others in a way that will at least potentially lead them closer to Christ through the preaching and teaching of the gospel message.

43

In the latter part of the first section of this verse we further see that this individual who is un-righteously selfish in fact is not only selfish, then being so he breaks out against all sound judgment, that is he acts and thinks in an irrational manner. As related to apologetics this shows us that we must refrain from selfish motives when interacting with those who oppose our beliefs, for in doing so we defeat the very purpose of Christian apologetics which is to prove the rationality of the Christian worldview. Furthermore as we go through the remainder of this passage we see that a fool takes no pleasure in understanding, but rather is only merely concerned with telling people what he himself thinks. Again this shows us that we must be careful in doing apologetics not to simply state our opinions, for in doing so we only prove ourselves to be fools. Instead we must be concerned with being rational, truthful, honest, and forthright with the facts and the evidence, rather than our own opinions, for in presenting our mere opinions we ultimately convey nothing more than what we think, whereas in presenting facts and evidence in an honest and trustworthy manner we lead people closer to the truth, which ultimately, if done properly in the context of true apologetics which is evangelical and evangelistic in nature, will lead them closer to Christ.

Proverbs 18:17

"The one who states his case first seems right, until the other comes and examines him."

In this particular passage we see that the first one to speak in a given situation thinks himself to be right, or rather seems to be right, until another person comes along and questions him. This shows us in general that virtually everyone who speaks without being questioned is going to assume that they are correct due to the lack of being questioned. This is a problem primarily because often times as fallen human beings we do not see things as they really are, that is we are often mistaken in our beliefs and assertions, at least initially. This means that we should be careful not only to question what we hear others say but also what we ourselves would say if we had the opportunity and the desire to do so. This does not mean that we need to be total skeptics, but a healthy level of skepticism when kept in check is definitely a positive thing to embrace. This is because the truth is often hidden from us at first glance and must be drawn out through adequate study via looking into things for ourselves.

There is one more thing that needs to be understood regarding this passage. It is important for us to remember that when we are speaking to others that disagree with us and our beliefs, often times the one whom we are speaking to has not adequately questioned his or her own beliefs and assertions, but nevertheless as this passage indicates they will think that they are correct. This is yet another reason why we must question them in their beliefs out-rightly, for doing so may cause them to potentially doubt and/or question their beliefs and in doing so we may very well lead them to reconsider and possibly even ultimately embrace a Christian worldview in the end.

Proverbs 23:9

"Do not speak in the hearing of a fool, for he will despise the good sense of your words."

Now in the first part of this passage we see that we are not to speak where fools can hear us, or rather in the presence of one who is properly labeled a fool. This does not mean that we are not to speak to a fool at all at any time and in any sense, but rather only when he is acting as such, that is as a fool. This is because, as the second part of the verse indicates, he who is truly a fool will simply despise what you say, especially if you are speaking the truth, or at least if you are speaking in a rational and coherent manner. Also this passage indicates that the speaking that is being referred to in the first part of this verse has to do with coherent dialogue, rather than referring to all speaking in general. This does not however mean that you cannot simply ask the question "why?" To ask this question is to make the fool at the very least think about his own foolishness in his own words and in his own mind rather than to think about a particular argument or assertion that you yourself are making to them. So, when we are speaking to someone who obviously is not concerned with the truth and one who does not as noted above heed the commandments of God, it is best to simply ask questions that cause them to think about their own beliefs and to articulate their own beliefs rather than to tell them about the various evidences that would ordinarily lead someone closer to the truth.

Proverbs 26:4

"Answer not a fool according to his folly, lest you be like him yourself."

This passage is very similar in a certain sense to the previous passage discussed above, but it has some distinctiveness to it nonetheless. In this passage we see that we are not to answer a fool according to his folly, that is, we are not to respond to a fool as a fool ourselves. This is because, as the second part of the verse states, by doing so we become a fool ourselves. But what does it mean to answer a fool as a fool? It seems best to answer this question by simply saying that to answer a fool in a way that is indicative of his own foolishness, or rather his own incoherent and/or irrational belief system or assertions is to yourself become irrational and incoherent in a certain sense. So how are we to respond to a fool if not according to his own folly? Well, the opposite of

49

responding to someone in a foolish manner would be to respond rather in a coherent and rational manner, primarily through speaking the truth through presenting various facts and evidences, and ultimately by leading them closer to Christ in some form or fashion, as that is ultimately the purpose of apologetics as stated above.

Proverbs 29:22

"A man of wrath stirs up strife, and one given to anger causes much transgression."

In this final passage of this chapter we see that someone who is prone to unrighteous anger tends to cause strife or grief that results from quarrels. We also see here that an "angry person" causes not only strife but transgressions. The difference between strife and transgressions is that strife is primarily, as stated above, a sort of grief or anxiety that results from various types of dissension or unwelcome argumentation, while transgressions are actually more equivalent to sins, or that which goes against God's commandments or nature. So we see here that in no way does presenting oneself in a manner that is consistent with being considered an angry person, or rather as one who is angry without good reason or who aims one's anger in an appropriate manner or fashion, lend one's situation to a positive outcome. We must remember this when dealing with others, especially when confronting others in their irrationality regarding religious and philosophical issues, for by presenting ourselves as less than meek and humble we thereby, even if inadvertently so, lend the situation to a less than desirable outcome to put it lightly, and we may even lead the individual who is opposing us and our beliefs even further away from Christ in the end.

Practical Take-a-ways

- We must heed God's commands.

- We must not isolate ourselves.

- We must avoid simply sharing our opinion.

- Remember that everyone thinks their beliefs are correct until questioned.

- We must maintain rational and coherent dialogues.

Chapter 5: Romans 12:17-19 and 14:18-19

"Repay no one evil for evil, but give thought to do what is honorable in the sight of all. [18] If possible, so far as it depends on you, live peaceably with all. [19] Beloved, never avenge yourselves, but leave it to the wrath of God, for it is written, "Vengeance is mine, I will repay, says the Lord." – Romans 12:17-19 (ESV)

"Whoever thus serves Christ is acceptable to God and approved by men. [19] So then let us pursue what makes for peace and for mutual upbuilding." – Romans 14:18-19 (ESV)

In the book of Romans we see a number of principles that deal specifically with interacting with people, especially those who interact with us in a manner that is considered to be "evil." This is an important issue to consider, as many times while endeavoring in the apologetic task we come across those who are, let us say, less than sympathetic to our views, and we must remember when interacting with these people that we have a responsibility not only to our fellow believers and to the individuals with whom we are speaking but also to Christ as to how we communicate the message of truth.

Romans 12:17-19

"Repay no one evil for evil, but give thought to do what is honorable in the sight of all. [18] If possible, so far as it depends on you, live peaceably with all. [19] Beloved, never avenge yourselves, but leave it to the wrath of God, for it is written, "Vengeance is mine, I will repay, says the Lord."

The first part of verse 17 in the book of Romans is pretty straightforward, namely do not repay evil for evil, that is, when one interacts with you in a manner that is not consistent with God's nature and commandments do not respond likewise but rather react in a way that pleases Christ and shows that you honor and obey Him and His teachings. Also in the second part of verse 17 we see that we are to be careful to do what is honorable not only in our own sight but in the sight of all. Now this obviously does not mean "all" in the sense of every single man and what he believes to be right, for seldom do men agree on what is truly right, and so it is impossible to completely generalize the idea of honorable with regard to every single person. Rather in the context of Scripture we are to view this passage as commanding us to ultimately do what is right and honorable in the eyes of those who concur with Christ, for those who are in line with Christ and his teachings are ultimately those who are honorable in the first place, and who understand honor to begin with.

In the second verse of this passage we see that we are to live at peace with everyone as much as possible. We also see that, by the very nature of the fact that the verse starts with the phrase "if possible," and that is followed by the phrase "so far as it depends on you," it is unlikely that this will always be the case, that is, that we will always be able to live peaceably with everyone. In fact we see time and time again in life that it is often not possible to live at peace, and this is ultimately due to the sin that is in the world and in each one of us. Nevertheless as the passage states, we are to live in peace as far as it depends on us rather than as far as it depends on others, and so we must take care to do whatever is necessary to be humble, trustworthy, honest, and meek, and anything else that would lend others to live at peace with us, for to some extent whether or not others are able to live at peace with us is dependent on our interactions with them.

In verse 19 of this passage we also see that we are not to avenge ourselves. This is because it is God's job and not ours to defend us, as ultimately when people offend us and our Christianity they are offending Him, and He is far more important than we are in the grand scheme of things. We would all do well to remember this when we come across those certain individuals who just, quite simply, really get under our skin. We need to maintain an awareness of the fact that our fight, as stated in an earlier chapter of this book, is not with man but with the devil and his demons, and that is a battle that

we certainly cannot win on our own. Therefore it is best

as this passage says to let God do the avenging, as only

He can truly do in such circumstances.

Romans 14:18-19

"Whoever thus serves Christ is acceptable to God and approved by men. [19] So then let us pursue what makes for peace and for mutual upbuilding."

Here in Romans 14:18 we see that he who serves Christ,

that is he who follows God's commands and does not

conform to this world but rather seeks to further the

gospel message in the teachings of Jesus, is acceptable to

God. What does it mean to be acceptable to God? To be

blunt it means to be right. This is an important

observation to make when considering the task of

argumentation involved in apologetics, for so often we

wish to be right, but in our own right and for our own

sake, rather than in a way that pleases Christ and serves

to further His glory. This verse brings home the reality that when we seek to be right but fail to serve Christ in the process, then ultimately regarding the things that truly matter we are indeed wrong nonetheless. This verse also tells us that he who serves Christ is approved by men. This obviously does not mean that all men will approve of Christians when they are acting as such, but rather it means that man in general is sympathetic to the characteristics of the type of individual who lives as Christ has called us to live, such as to be humble, compassionate, honest, and the like.

In the latter verse of this passage we see the continuation of thought from verse 18 in which Paul tells us that we are, due to the nature of serving Christ, to pursue that which brings about peace and mutual encouragement. This means that we are not only to be humble, compassionate, honest and so on, but also that we are to strive to be pleasant, empathetic, and encouraging at the very least. This idea resonates strongly with the passage in 1 Peter 3:15-16 where the apostle Peter tells us that we are to interact with people in a loving and kind manner, including and especially when we are defending the faith.

Practical Take-a-ways

- Never avenge yourself; that is God's job.

- Remember that our fight is not with humanity but with Satan and his demons.

- As much as possible we are to live at peace with everyone.

- We are to seek to further Christ and His glory in the process of doing apologetics.

- We are to be humble, meek, compassionate, trustworthy, honest, and empathetic when interacting with others.

Chapter 6: Tying It All Together

Now that we have had a chance to go through these various passages in a bit of exegetical depth, it is time to tie the various practical take away principles together in a way that fully establishes the basis for the biblical principles that I am setting forth in this book as the basis for what I call "confrontational relationality," that is, interacting with people in a way that is confrontational and yet still breeds legitimate and healthy relationships. Throughout this final chapter, therefore, we will basically be putting the various practical aspects of each of the previous chapters together so that we can better understand these principles within the bigger picture.

First and foremost we are to be bold and necessary. Again this does not mean that we need to be arrogant or disrespectful, but it is absolutely vital that we stand firm on the gospel message and truth in general, for truth stems from the very nature and essence of God, and the gospel message is the crux of the Christian faith. So the next time you feel like breaking down from argument or being timid when confronted with opposition to faith and beliefs remember that you are called and commanded in the Scriptures to be bold for the sake and cause of Christ.

Next, we are to be humble always, but not merely humble, but also meek, compassionate, trustworthy, honest, empathetic, and anything else that personifies Christ in his nature. We also need to remember that in being humble and such we must never forget, as stated in the previous paragraph, that we are to maintain a certain level of boldness in all that we say and do, standing firmly on the gospel message and the Scriptures as they are truly the basis of our faith. We must also be careful as to how we speak, remembering that either we curse through our speech or we bless through our speech, but we cannot do both at the same time in the same sense. Blessings cannot breed evil, and curses cannot breed goodness, at least not in the sense spoken of here, for here, to curse is to condemn and to bless is to uphold or uplift. We also must remember as we interact with people that at least until they are questioned about their beliefs they are most likely to assume that they are correct, which gives us all the more reason to question them in the first place.

Third, we must never forget that our fight is not with humanity, but rather it is with Satan and his demons. This is a very important point, for oftentimes we get caught up in the moment of arguments and we forget that we are not fighting with the individual standing across from us but rather with those who are responsible for the daemonic influence so involved therein that is causing them to deny the faith and cling to evil. We are to love people, all people, and hate sin.

Fourth, it is absolutely vital that we never forget as believers that it is ultimately the Holy Spirit who is responsible and able to bring people to a saving knowledge of Jesus Christ. It is one thing to argue and to defend the gospel message and the intellectual validity of Christianity as a worldview and religion, it is quite another to think that we actually have the ability to save people within ourselves. The purpose of apologetics is to lead people to Christ and this too must never be forgotten, for all too many have gone out into the world to win yet another argument while forgetting that the far more important task is to "win the soul." We are to always first and foremost seek to further Christ and his glory and message in the process of doing apologetics, for in doing this the Lord may well bring our opponents to a saving knowledge of him through the work of his Holy Spirit by the use of us as human beings to break down the mental walls and barriers that keep so many people from accepting Christianity and coming to know Christ as Lord. It is certainly true that Christianity and becoming a Christian is more than a lack of intellectual skepticism about the faith, but nevertheless such skepticism certainly does hinder many individuals from coming to Christ. Finally, regarding this fourth point, we must never forget that all Christians must not only be willing but able to teach and to teach at minimum the gospel message, for to fail to do so is to fail to live up to even the minimalist of expectations from our Lord via the Great Commission.

Fifth, we must be kind to everyone no matter how

they treat us. It is absolutely vital to one's own personal walk with Christ as well as Christendom as a whole that we live in peace with everyone as far as it is possible through us, for to fail to be peaceable on purpose and principle is to fail to be Christian in practice and participation. Let us also be patient in our endurance of evil of all types, especially the evil that is set before us when certain people so vehemently oppose us, sometimes even to the extent of verbally and/or physically abusing us, or even torturing or killing us as so often we forget happens in various parts of the world. We must always heed God's commands, including the command to not bear false witness against your neighbor such as was discussed earlier in this book. We must also remember that God's commands extend far beyond the 10 Commandments and that everything that is said in the Scriptures to be conducive of the Christian walk in faith is essentially a commandment given by God to His people. Finally, we must not isolate ourselves from others, but rather we must embrace the task of apologetics and evangelism and go out into the world and do whatever we can to lead people to Christ, for without Christ they truly have no hope.

Sixth, we must completely avoid worthless discussions and all types of quarrels that breed nothing more than nonsense and dissension. We must maintain rational and coherent dialogues and speak to people in a way that is not only intelligent but also in a way that they can understand, for to speak in a way that seems intelligent but is ultimately not understandable to the individual with whom you are speaking is to ultimately be unintelligible, and to be

unintelligible is ultimately to partake in worthless discussion, which we have established is completely unacceptable within the Christian faith. We also must avoid simply sharing our opinions, but instead we must be careful to share what is true and what is right and what is just and what is noble and what is fact to the best of our knowledge and ability so as to lead people closer to the truth with the T, that is to the Truth that is Christ. We must also be careful to remember to oppose those who oppose us by correcting them so that through that correction they may reevaluates their own system of beliefs and hopefully come to know Christ as Lord in the end, which also requires prayer, which must never be forgotten as one of the most vital roles and necessities of the Christian. Finally, we must always remember never to avenge ourselves as that is God's job, not ours!

Seventh, in all this we must remember that all people, Christian and non-Christian alike, are made in the image of God, and therefore share in the inherent dignity that has been bestowed on all humans. This means that we must be careful, nay, very careful how we interact with fellow human beings whether or not they agree with our positions and beliefs, which is one of the reasons that I am writing this book in hopes that those who read it will come to a fuller understanding of what the Bible teaches about how we are to interact with others, especially those who disagree with us that we are likely to forget share in such dignity.

In closing, I pray that each and every one of you that reads this book gain a much better understanding of how God calls us to do apologetics. It is not simply a game of argumentation and wits, but rather it is evangelism in the strictest sense of the term. As Paul says in the book of Romans, if we do not go to those who do not believe, then how can they ever believe? The answer is an emphatic "they cannot!" And so we must be careful in our endeavor to go to these lost people of the world, and embrace these biblical principles for a confrontational relationality in the process, for doing so we are destined to lead far more people closer to Christ than if we abandon and ignore such biblical principles.

In Christ,

Trevor Ray Slone

www.ingramcontent.com/pod-product-compliance
Lightning Source LLC
Chambersburg PA
CBHW071847020426
42331CB00007B/1901